To Mandy —
Thanks for coming to
see us! Enjoy —
Lori Ellen Hooft ☺

Linda R. Peckham

10/16/99

Saw Mills and Sleigh Bells

Stories of Mid-Michigan Settlers

Linda R. Peckham and Lori Ellen Heuft

Catalpa Publications
Williamston, Michigan 48895
May 1999

Saw Mills and Sleigh Bells: Stories of Mid-Michigan Settlers
ISBN 0-9671616-1-4
Library of Congress Catalog Card Number: 99-62897
May 1999

Cover Illustration by Robert Morris
Cover Design and Production by Loretta Crum
Technical Support and Photo Reproduction by Jerry Heuft
Photos not otherwise credited are property of the authors

We dedicate this work to the pioneers
whose lives gave us this legacy,
and to the children
who will make tomorrow's history.

History continues to be discovered, and we would like to acknowledge the many people who provided assistance:

Professor Emeritus Robert Bandurski, Botany, Michigan State University; Val Berryman and Terry Shaffer, Michigan State University Museum; Kerry Chartkoff, Capitol Archives; Dr. George Cornell, Urban Affairs, Michigan State University; David Jones, Friends of Historic Williamstown; Jim McLean, Lansing Library; Virginia Schlichter, Mason Historical Society; Professor Morris Thomas, Geography, Lansing Community College; Tom Weise, Elaine Carlson, Dave Kenyon, Department of Natural Resources; Woldumar Nature Center; Cameron Wood, Nokomis; Jane Woolsey, Meridian Historic Village.

The Historical Society of Greater Lansing, especially Rick Cantwell; David Caterino; John Curry, State Archives, Ret.; Pat Heyden; Ben Kidder; Jerry Lawler; Jane McClary, Local History Librarian, Ret.; Fr. George Michalek, Archivist, Diocese of Lansing; Robert Morris; Craig Whitford; Geneva Wiskemann.

Dick and Shirley Bradley, George Fogle, Howard Gorsline, Betty Keitchen, Joy Peterson, Lennah Preuss, Andra Scott Price, Suzanne Ballard Sell, Phil Siebert, June Stover, Ingrid Vedder, Richard Wheeler, Naomi Whitmyer, Ruth Wright.

Carmen Benavides, Principal, Reo Elementary, Lansing; Pam Hawkins, Waverly Schools; Sue Austin, teacher, Williamston; and all of their students.

The Skaaldic Society, a writers group; Jennifer, Michael, and Heather Heuft, Jacqueline Laba, Matthew and Kelsie Peckham, and Nicole Searles, our young editors.

Jerry Heuft and Robert Morris, for their ideas and continued support.

CONTENTS

Illustrations

Chief Okemos: Before the Settlers

Before any white settlers set foot in mid-Michigan, the grandfathers of Chief Okemos hunted, fished, and raised their children here.

Okemos was born about 1775, in the camp of his father on the Shiawassee River, near Bancroft. He grew up during a time of fierce conflict between the new Americans and the Indians. They had different beliefs about the land.

> Bancroft is between Lansing and Flint. A historical marker about the old Indian settlement, "Ketchewandaugoning," stands at Knaggs Bridge.

The Indians believed the land was a gift from one of their gods. She sent them animals and rain so they could survive. They hunted, built villages, and planted corn on the land. They *used* the land, but they believed no one *owned* the land.

When the new American settlers came to the Midwest, they said they *owned* the land. They said they won it from the British in the Revolutionary War, and they would not let the Indians use the land. Because of these different beliefs, many battles were fought.

> The land by the Great Lakes was called the Northwest Territory. For 40 years, the Indians and new Americans fought over who should live there.

Okemos was a brave fighter in these battles. From 1791 to 1814, he fought against the Americans in several major battles in Ohio, Indiana, and southeast Michigan.

In the War of 1812, the Indians and the British fought together against the Americans. In one terrible battle, Okemos got a bad skull wound, wide enough to lay three fingers in. In another battle, in Canada, Okemos fought alongside the famous warrior, Tecumseh. Okemos was wounded again; Tecumseh was killed.

> Battles did not take place in mid-Michigan, because no Americans lived there yet.

This battle was the last attempt to keep the Americans out of the Midwest. The British and Indians had lost the war.

In 1814, Okemos was among those who signed a peace treaty in Detroit. Okemos said, "Now I make peace and fight no more. *Chemokemon* too much for Indians. Me fight plenty enough."

The Indians had to give up the land, and most were moved to reservations by the United States government. Okemos, though, stayed near his father's old camp on the Shiawassee River.

In the 1830s, smallpox and cholera killed many of the Indians who remained. Okemos became the chief of a small, mixed group of Indian families, from the Ottawa, Potawatomi, and Chippewa tribes. In his own family, Okemos had a daughter, two sons, and grandchildren. His cousin became a chief of another mixed group nearby.

Only a few Indian villages were ever located near Lansing. There were four villages near Williamston and Okemos, three near Stockbridge, and three near Grand Ledge. Clinton County had only five villages.

> Most of the Michigan Indians lived along the Great Lakes or in Southern Michigan. Jackson County had 23 Indian villages.

The Indian men hunted deer, rabbit, and pheasant

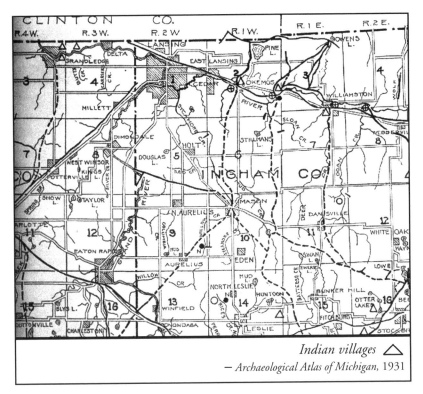

Indian villages △
— *Archaeological Atlas of Michigan*, 1931

with bow and arrow. They speared salmon in the rivers. In the late winter, they collected sap from the maple trees to make maple syrup and candy.

They ate nuts from the hickory trees and wild fruits from the meadows: plum, crabapple, grape, strawberry, blackberry. Everything was shared.

In the summers, the Indians prepared planting grounds, where they grew corn, beans, and squash. They mounded up the dirt about a foot high in long rows and planted seeds in these hills. In between the rows, they let the grasses grow.

> One planting ground was at Ferguson Park, in Okemos.

Near the planting grounds, the Indians dug caves in the riverbanks, lined them with bark,

> Some caves were found on the Red Cedar River between Okemos and Williamston.

and stored corn and dried venison for the winter.

The Indians also kept burial grounds. They felt very close to their ancestors who died. To remember the dead, they held a ceremony each year and left food for them at their graves.

> Burial grounds are known near Okemos, Portland, and Dimondale.

When the new settlers arrived in mid-Michigan in the 1830s, the Indians were friendly and helpful. When a settler was lost in the woods, the Indians knew where to find the trail. When he was sick with ague, the Indians knew what roots and herbs would make him well.

> Ague (a-gyoo) was an illness related to malaria.

Indian men helped the settlers build their log cabins. The women helped each other sew. Children played and fished together.

Chief Okemos often gave presents to the children of the settlers. He gave a tiny, woven basket filled with corn to baby Mary Sherman. It was a rattle for her to shake. Two of the Chief's grandsons gave a real canoe to Dan Mevis, a boy who visited the Indian camp many times. It was a very light, dug-out canoe made of walnut, just the right size for one boy to ride in.

Rattle box
Given to Mary
Sherman, b. 1851
– From Michigan
State University
Museum

Because of bad memories, though, some settlers were afraid of the Indians. But Chief Okemos, the old warrior, had promised never to fight again.

He never broke his promise.

Chief Okemos died on December 5, 1858, when he was about 85 years old. His body was buried with his tobacco pouch and his bullet bag at Shimnecon, on the Grand River near Portland.

In 1859, the village known as Hamilton was renamed Okemos in his honor.

Chief Okemos
— Local History Room, Lansing Library

In 1923, over 2,000 school children in Ingham, Clinton, Ionia, and Shiawassee counties helped raise money for a marker to remember Chief Okemos. The marker is on Central Elementary School, Okemos.

A team of oxen standing in their yoke
An adult ox can weigh 3,000 pounds. Settlers relied on the great strength
of their oxen for hauling wagons, logs, and plowing fields.
– Tillers International, Kalamazoo, Michigan

Putnams' Attempt

The forest was thick in Ingham County in the spring of 1834. Two brothers walked a few steps and stopped again. Raising their axes up over their shoulders, they took aim, and chopped at the huge trees. The sound echoed around them. A few feet at a time, swinging and chopping, the brothers worked hard all day to clear a trail wide enough for their two oxen and wagon to travel on.

Hiram and Joseph Putnam were eager to be pioneers. They came from the town of Jackson, and were going north to start a new settlement along the Cedar River. On the way, they had met the only other white man in Ingham county. His name was David Rodgers, and he was building a cabin in a place we now call Stockbridge. Then they started chopping.

> The Cedar River later became known as the Red Cedar River.

At night, Hiram and Joseph built a campfire and ate turnips, or cooked a pheasant they had shot. It took weeks to make the new trail. When they reached the Cedar River, their trail was twenty miles long.

> How far is 20 miles? Pioneer trails had hills, stumps, bumps, and were very hard to walk or ride on. It took all day for a wagon to travel 20 miles. How long do you think it would take today, if you were riding in a car?

On the north side of the river, the brothers found a large clearing. Slowly and carefully, they led the oxen and wagon into the chilly water and waded across. They built a log cabin in the clearing, 12 feet wide and 16 feet long.

> Is your living room bigger or smaller than the Putnam cabin?

Hiram and Joseph wanted to be farmers, but life was not easy in the wilderness. They worked hard every day, chopping trees and plowing the ground. There were Indians living in the area with their leader, Chief Okemos, but there were no other settlers nearby. The brothers became lonesome for their family, friends, and comforts of home.

> Does your car weigh more or less than an ox?

Then one day the oxen wandered off into the woods wearing their yoke. A yoke kept the animals together so they could work as a team and pull heavy loads.

The oxen were lost for days, and when the brothers found them, one had died from hunger. The other had been dragging its partner around the woods searching for food, and it was not much more than bones. It died, too.

Now there were no animals to help with the farm work. Hiram and Joseph Putnam left their log cabin and went back to Jackson.

Five years later, in 1839, three brothers decided to leave their parents and sisters in New York state to "go west." Their names were Oswald, J.M., and Horace Williams. Like the Putnams, the Williams brothers wanted adventure. They had heard that Michigan was a beautiful place full of trees and blue lakes, with lots of land for sale.

> Michigan became a state in 1837. How many states are there in the United States today? What number was Michigan?

They traveled by stage coach, then steamboat, to a city called Detroit. From there they walked 70 miles, to the spot where the Putnams had lived. They bought the land and built a new log cabin in the spring of 1840.

One rainy autumn day, the Williams brothers were visited by two men who were driving a wagon to Grand Rapids. The men were soaked to the skin, and glad to find the cabin. They had seen light from the fireplace shining through the window openings.

Williams brothers' first home
— Pencil sketch by Crary Grattan, 1856
First published in the *Williamston Enterprise*, October, 1891.

Settlers were always happy to help a weary traveler, because people lived so far apart. They enjoyed having company, too. Visitors brought the news from other places.

The men hung their wet coats by the fire. There were no extra chairs, so one man took an axe from the wagon and chopped blocks of wood for stools.

Supper was cooked in a big black kettle, hanging over the fire from the log-pole in the chimney. When it was ready, they used two barrels for a table. Everyone enjoyed the hot mush and milk. The visitors thought it was as good as any food they could get in the city.

That night, the visitors slept on the floor in front of the fireplace. In the morning, after breakfast of venison and coffee, they went on their way.

Later that year, Mr. Williams, the father of the settlers, came from New York to help build a dam across the river. This gave water power to the first saw mill, also built by the Williams men. By that time, more settlers had come. The brothers helped people clear the land for miles around, and logs became lumber in their mill. Now people could build houses of boards instead of logs.

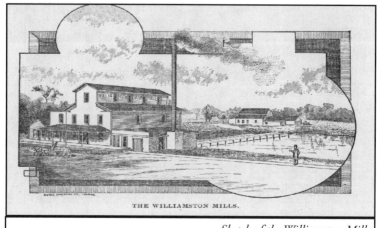

Sketch of the Williamston Mills
— Friends of Historic Williamstown

In 1842, they built a grist mill. Their father came again, and went to Detroit to get a mill stone. Now, local farmers did not need to go to Dexter, a three-day trip, to grind their grain into flour.

Soon there was a growing village, with a blacksmith shop, general store, bank, and post office. After a few years,

Quartz mill stone
McCormick Park,
Williamston

Oswald and Horace Williams moved to other towns. J.M. (James Miles) Williams stayed, got married, and raised a family. He helped his neighbors, and was admired as a wise and honest man. Years later, in 1871, the village that grew around him was officially named Williamston.

James Miles and Julia Carr Williams
− Friends of Historic Williamstown

Even though the Putnam brothers didn't stay, the trail they had cut through the forest was called the Putnam Trail. Today it is known by two names − Putnam Street and Williamston Road. It is the main road going north and south through the town of Williamston.

> Many roads were named after people. Do you know how the road you live on got its name?

2

The Giant Tic-Tac-Toe

Josiah looked around for the hundreth time, puzzled. "I have a question, Papa. How will we find our land?"

Jesse Munro flicked the reins over the oxen. "What do you mean?"

"Well, here we are on this wagon, and all I see are trees and the back ends of Ollie and Oscar. We left Detroit seven days ago. This land all looks the same to me." He shaded his eyes with his hand and looked around again. "If you've never seen our land, how will we know when we get there?"

His father chuckled. "Oh, it's easy, Josiah. Right underneath the wagon is a huge invisible map."

Josiah frowned. "A map on the ground?"

"Yep," his father said. "This invisible map has lines like a . . . like a giant tic-tac-toe."

Josiah still frowned.

"I'll show you," his father said. He stopped the oxen and told Josiah to hop down.

With a stick, Mr. Munro drew a big tic-tac-toe in the dirt. He told Josiah to stand at the lower right corner, outside the game.

"Pretend your land is in the upper right square of the tic-tac-toe. See it? Walk to your land."

Josiah took two giant steps forward. "That was easy," he said.

"Now go back to your starting place," his father said. "This time, pretend your land is in the second square left and the second square forward."

Josiah took two giant steps left and two giant steps forward. "Easy again," he said.

"And that is how we'll find our land," his father said. "Men called surveyors are measuring all of the land in Michigan. They measure it and mark it into hundreds of giant tic-tac-toes."

"Wow! All of Michigan? How long did that take?"

"Oh, they are not done. They are still measuring the northern part. They just got this part measured. That's why I could buy it."

Michigan, 1839
It took 50 years to survey all of Michigan.
– Michigan Road
  Builders Association

Land cost about $1.25 per acre in 1836 when Jesse Munro (Jessie Monroe) moved his family of nine "out west" from Buffalo, New York.

He had fought on the side of the Americans in the War of 1812, but in Michigan he and Chief Okemos became friends.

He pulled a cloth map out of his pocket. "See? Each square is called a township, and they give it a name. Our land is in Eagle Township in Clinton County. We'll be a few miles past DeWitt."

Josiah studied the map and then looked off to the north. "Could I be a surveyor, Papa? What do they do?"

"Oh, the surveyors are brave and strong men, Josiah. They live in the wilderness for weeks at a time, camping in tents. They get wet in the swamps, and tired from chopping down trees that are in their way. They have to carry all of their food and equipment with them."

"I can do that," Josiah said. "How do they measure the townships?"

"The surveyors use a compass, a chain, and a pole. One man sets up the compass. Another man stretches out the chain – a chain is 66 feet long. At the end of the chain, the man holds up the pole."

Why did they carry a chain instead of a long ruler? Chains are still used today in football games, to measure the distance to a first down.

Surveyor's Compass and Chain
– From Michigan State University Museum

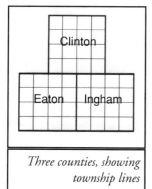

Three counties, showing township lines

His father held up an imaginary pole. "Then the two men line up the compass and the pole in a straight line. Every six miles, the surveyors pound a marker into the ground to show the corners of the squares – the new townships."

His father told him that in the East, they measured lines between rocks and trees. When the trees fell down or the rocks were moved, they lost their markers. There were many arguments about who owned the land. To measure out the squares was a new method.

"All of the squares in Michigan are measured from one single corner," his father said. "The starting corner was made where the first two important lines crossed each other. It's not far from us."

He pointed off into the trees. "The first north-south line is called the meridian. The first east-west line is called the base line, at the south edge of Eaton and Ingham Counties."

He explained that to make the base line, some of the surveyors started at Lake Michigan and measured east toward the meridian line. Other surveyors started near Detroit and measured west toward the meridian line.

Meridian and Base Lines
– Professor Morris Thomas

9

His father chuckled. "The surveyors," he said, "always tried to measure very straight lines. But when they reached the meridian line from each direction, they didn't match!"

> They were off by over 900 feet. You can see the jog today if you cross Meridian Road on Holt Road or Howell Road.

"What did they do?" Josiah asked.

"They had to draw a jog on the maps!"

As they got back on the wagon, Mr. Munro said, "Maybe someday, those township lines will become straight roads. For now, we'll just follow the old Indian trails."

He clucked at the oxen to make them go. "We should make it to Dr. Laing's tonight."

"Do you think his oxen," Josiah asked, "will drag the logs for the fireplace right into the cabin, like that first place we stayed?"

> Dr. Peter Laing founded Laingsburg in 1836.

His father chuckled, remembering. "I don't think his cabin will be that big, Josiah."

Mr. Munro looked at the sky. "If it doesn't rain, by tomorrow night we should be at DeWitt." He paused, thinking. "We'll leave your mother and sisters and the baby at Mr. Scott's for a few days until we build a cabin. I've been told he already has a big log house. We'll ask Mr. Scott to help us measure to our land in Eagle Township."

> DeWitt was settled in 1833 by Captain David Scott of Ann Arbor.

Josiah smiled as he looked around at the wide countryside. "Just like on a giant tic-tac-toe!"

> Today, when the astronauts fly in outer space, they can see two things on Earth: the Great Wall of China, and the squares made by the township line roads in the Midwest.

Ingham, Eaton, and Clinton Counties

City Lot   = 1 chain x 2-1/2 chains (Lansing, Original Plat)
                     (66' x 165')

80 chains   = 1 mile

1 mile x 1 mile   = 1 Section
                     Full section = 640 acres
                     Half section = 320 acres
                     Quarter section = 160 acres
                     Eighth section = 80 acres

36 Sections   = 1 Township (6 miles x 6 miles)

16 Townships   = 1 County

3

Mrs. Potter's Farm

It had only been a year since Linus Potter and his family settled in Eaton County. Suddenly, in the summer of 1846, Linus died. Mrs. Potter was left with seven children and an 80 acre farm to care for. Her brothers wanted her to move the family to New York, where they lived.

But Mrs. Potter was tired of moving. The family had already moved fifteen times. Linus had often been away from home, working as a surveyor. His widow knew how to take care of things by herself. As long as she could keep her children with her, she was determined to stay put. They decided to try it for one year.

The family already had a large log cabin, and a very nice frame barn. Linus had taken tamarack logs to the saw mill at Eaton Rapids, to be cut into lumber for building the barn. It measured 30 feet by 40 feet.

Early frame barn

George and Theodore were the oldest boys. They knew that the farm work would be up to them now. There would be no time for schooling.

Their first job was to cut down more trees, so they could have ten acres for planting wheat. George arranged to trade work with two men, so there was extra help with the logging.

> Trading work was very common. The settlers helped each other clear the forest, build cabins and barns, and harvest crops.

To get stumps out of the fields, George borrowed a stump puller, and hitched up the oxen to it. With Theodore's help, they pulled thirty or forty stumps each day. Soon the fields were smooth and bare.

Stump puller
— Joy Peterson

The family needed meat, and George did most of the hunting. There were plenty of deer, rabbit, pheasant, turkeys and quail in the woods. They also raised some hogs and cows.

One day, Theodore, who was fourteen, went into the woods to drive home the cows. The family dog trotted beside him. Suddenly, a large buck appeared, and went after them with his hooves and antlers!

Theodore dodged in and out of trees as the deer chased him. The dog snapped at the deer's legs. When the deer turned to chase the dog, Theodore picked up a big oak limb. He hit the deer very hard on its head. The deer fell to the ground, and died. Theodore went home and told George what had happened. They went back to the woods together and dragged the deer home. The family ate venison for a whole week.

Theodore sometimes worked away from home, too. He once helped a team of surveyors who were surveying a new road. For twenty-five cents a day, he carried water, made the campfire, and did some hunting to help feed the men. Another time, he helped build a log schoolhouse. Chief Okemos was camped nearby, and noticed one day that Theodore was working bare footed. The chief gave him a pair of nicely beaded moccasins, which Theodore was very proud of.

The Potters also had sheep. Theodore clipped the wool, and the younger children picked out burrs and bits of grass. The dense wool was carded to take out the tangles and loosen it into long fibers. Mrs. Potter twisted the fibers into yarn on a spinning wheel. She often dyed the yarn different colors.

Spinning wheel and carding combs
— Margaret Schrepfer

The children collected things from nature to make dye. Even three-year old

James could help. Butternut shucks made brown dye, and peach tree leaves made yellow. Madder root made a long-lasting red dye. Mrs. Potter cooked them in water, and the color seeped out. She soaked the yarn in the colored water.

Mrs. Potter, Louise and Sarah knitted mittens, hats, stockings, and even suspenders from their homemade yarn. They also wove the yarn into heavy fabric on a loom, and made clothing. Thread and light fabric for dresses and shirts were bought from the general store.

The cow gave them milk and butter. The oldest sister, Louise, made butter by stirring and mashing cream from the milk in a butter churn. It took several hours of churning for the cream to thicken into butter. This was a job that ten-year-old Sarah liked to help with, even though it made her arms tired.

Sometimes the girls would go with their mother to a quilting bee. All the neighbor women would get together and bring scraps of fabric. They sang songs, told stories, and sewed all day.

At harvest time the first year, George and Theodore cut the ten acres of wheat with grain cradles. They walked up and down the fields, swinging the cradles. The cut wheat was fed into a threshing machine to

Grain cradle
— From Michigan State University Museum

Sketch of a horse-powered threshing machine
Manufactured by Nichols & Shepard, Battle Creek, Michigan
– Michigan State University Museum

separate the grain from the plant. The machine worked by horse power. They had 400 bushels of wheat when they were done.

With George managing the farm, and everyone helping, they got along just fine.

When she was eighty years old, Mrs. Potter wrote a letter to her grandson. She ended by saying, "I kept my family with me until they became men and women . . . and all have good homes and families." She was glad she had stayed.

The town of Potterville is named for this family, and the three boys in the story were especially well known.

George became Sheriff of Eaton County and a State Senator, as well as a director of the Peninsular (Grand Trunk) Railroad.

Theodore went west to find gold, fought in wars, and helped capture bank robbers! He settled in Vermontville, and laid out the town of Mulliken.

James had a furniture business in Lansing, and donated the land for Potter Park Zoo.

– 4 –

Mr. Seymour's Town

I am Joab Page and today is July 4, 1850. My grandson, Marshall Pease, is five years old, and when he is just a little older, I want to tell him some stories.

I want to tell Marshall that we were the first family to settle – and stay – in what is now Lansing. We moved here from Mason, and before that we lived in Jackson.

But before we came, some friends of mine from Jackson, Jerry and William Ford, tried to start a town here. In 1836, they invested in some land near the big south bend of the Grand River, planned a town, and named it "Biddle City." It was a good idea.

They went back to Tompkins County, New York, where they had grown up, and offered to sell the lots in the new town to their friends. Their friends in New York wanted to buy good land in Michigan.

Their friends came to "look the land" – but the river had overflowed in a flood. The land was under water! None of these men bought land in Biddle City.

Several of the men, though, bought farm land nearby – Mr. North, Mr. Ludlow, Mr. Buck, and others. They were neighbors in New York, and now they are neighbors here. My grandson knows them all.

Another man, Mr. James Seymour, also bought a lot of land in this section in 1836, and he also wanted to start a town. It would be like another town he started in

Michigan, called Flushing.

By 1843, not much was happening here, so Mr. Seymour decided to build a dam on the Grand River where the Indian trail touches it.

> Flushing is near Flint.

James Seymour
An investor from New York
– History of Flushing

Mr. Seymour hired John Burchard, a friend of mine from Mason and Jackson, to build the dam. John Burchard moved up here and built the dam and a log cabin for his family.

I suppose I should tell my grandson the rest of the story, too – when he's a little older.

You see, the next spring the dam leaked, and John went out in his boat to fix it. The rushing water turned his boat over, and John drowned. We couldn't believe it. We still feel very sad about this.

But Mr. Seymour still wanted a town. In 1844, he asked us to rebuild the broken dam. We told Mr. Seymour no one lived there, what did he need a dam for? He said people would come to live there if there was a dam.

> A plaque at Center Street and Grand River Avenue, North Lansing, marks the site of Burchard's cabin.

"The water power is strong at that site," he said. "I'll pay you to build a saw mill, too."

Well, we had built good dams and mills when we lived in Jackson. Then we moved to Mason and worked there. We knew what to do.

So several people in my family all moved a few miles north again. It took one whole day to travel the 14 miles from Mason.

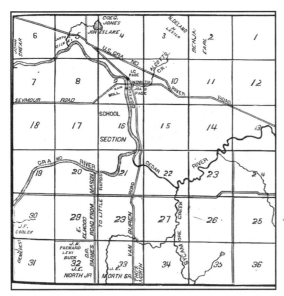

Lansing Township, 1845
– Eaton and Ingham
County History, 1880

We found the empty log cabin near the broken dam, but that's all there was. It was a pretty spot, though, with huge maple trees all around us and that beautiful big river just down the hill. We all shared the cabin, the women cooked outside, and we made do.

We hired everybody we could find to help fix the dam and build the saw mill. We paid fifty cents a day, a lot of money then.

> How much do people get paid today?

Of course, we had to give the workers a place to eat and sleep, so we added a section to the cabin. The downstairs room was the dining room; the upstairs room was the sleeping loft.

When visitors came by, they stayed with us, too. Then in 1846, we started a church class, and we met on Sundays in the dining room. That little cabin was our home, a boarding house, a hotel, and a church!

> This church class was Methodist, the first church group in Lansing.

After we built the saw mill, the farmers brought

their logs to us to be cut into planks, but people didn't move here to make a new town.

So Mr. Seymour made another plan. He knew that the governor of Michigan wanted to move the capital city from Detroit to the center of the state.

Some of the legislators wanted to move the capital to towns like Jackson or Marshall. Others wanted Owosso or Lyons or Calumet. But Mr. Seymour wanted it to be located here! In Lansing Township! In the wilderness!

> A "legislator" is a person who makes laws.

The legislators thought Mr. Seymour's idea was a joke. The railroad didn't come here. The roads didn't come here. There wasn't even a town! One legislator said, "What? Shall we take the capitol . . . and stick it down in the woods and mud on the bank of the Grand River?"

Mr. Seymour went to Detroit to talk to the legislators. He took a map of Michigan and a red pen. He drew big red lines on the map, pointing to Lansing Township.

He showed them that the land he owned was at the center of everything – the perfect place for the new capital city. Some legislators liked the idea.

The legislators voted and voted. They could not agree on any of the other towns, so they voted for Mr. Seymour's plan. In March of

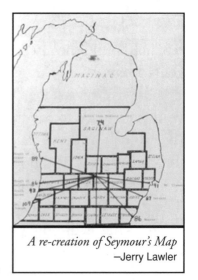

A re-creation of Seymour's Map
—Jerry Lawler

1847, our spot on the map became the capital of Michigan.

Mr. Seymour would finally get his town.

5

The Race to Michigan, Michigan

What a story I have to tell my grandson, Marshall Pease, when he's a little older. We were so happy when Lansing Township was chosen for the site of the new capital city in 1847, just three years ago.

But there was no town. We had to make a town! And it had to be ready to be the capital city in nine months!

> If you planned a town, what would you put in it?

This whole town was planned ahead of time. It would be two miles long and one mile wide. They named the new town "Michigan," Michigan.

Surveyors drew a plat map, to show us where all of the streets would be. They said to me, "Joab Page, your

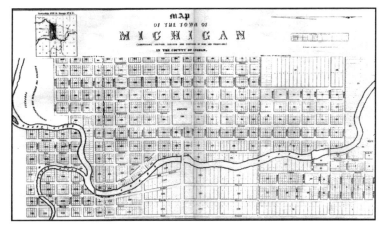

Plat Map of the Town of Michigan
A plat map shows the plan of a town.
– Historical Society of Greater Lansing

cabin was the first one here, so we'll call this Center Street."

They decided to build the capitol building about a mile south of our dam. Main Street was a few blocks south of that.

Some men from Eaton Rapids cut down the biggest tree they could find and dragged it through the woods to our sawmill. That's 18 miles! They said, "Cut it into boards and use it for the new capitol building." And we did.

People raced to build the new town. They knew business would be good. They built houses and hotels and grocery stores and blacksmith shops near the new capitol. They built a bridge across the river at Main Street. Mr. Peck opened a post office.

Rare postmark of Michigan, Mic.
– Craig Whitford

In our part of town, Mr. Seymour, the man who owned so much land, built a big hotel. We built a gristmill for Mr. Hiram Smith, a man I knew from Mason – and Jackson before that. Mr. James Turner, a man I also knew from Mason and Jackson, moved here and opened a general store. He sold shoes and pitch forks and just about everything.

Frame house of James and Marian Munro Turner, 1847
– Local History Room, Lansing Library

We built a second bridge, near the dam on Franklin Street. A second church was started. So many people settled here that we started a school. The first schoolhouse wasn't much. It was just a shanty with greased paper for a window. We built a better one in a few months.

> The first school stood on North Cedar Street, near Franklin Street (Grand River Ave.), the site of schools ever since.

Presbyterian Church, 1852
They started the second church group.
– Local History Room, Lansing Library

It was a frantic time. The hotels never had enough beds for all of the visitors and workers. One man told me he had to sleep on a chair for the first three weeks he was here. Lots of families let strangers stay overnight in their houses.

When my grandson is a little older, I'll have to tell him what the workers on the new capitol building did. After they cut down the trees where the capitol building would go, they played a game of "base ball." It's a new game, one I don't quite understand.

A man throws a ball to another man who tries to hit it with a stick. If he hits the ball, he runs toward a spot they have marked. If a field man catches the ball, at least on the first bounce, the hitter is out. If a field man picks up the ball, throws it at the hitter and hits him, the hitter is out. I'm not sure this game is going to last – it's pretty silly.

There's another story I have to tell my grandson, too. The state hired a man to move the papers up here from the old capitol building in Detroit. It takes at least 18 hours to get here from Detroit, and they wanted him to hurry.

He ran his horse hard. Too hard. He made it to the new capitol, but his horse fell down and died. The state had to pay the man $75 to buy a new horse.

Anyway, in just nine months, we built a whole town! It is amazing to see. Oh, the dirt streets are still full of tree stumps. And all of those horses stink the place up. And the creek just north of the capitol is a muddy problem. But overall, it's a good little town.

Washington Avenue, c. 1860
– Local History Room, Lansing Library

When the legislators met here for the first time in January of 1848, we were ready. The capitol is such a pretty building. With its green shutters and a cupola on the roof, it looks very stately.

We changed the name of the town to "Lansing"

The 1847 Capitol
A model of the 1847 Capitol was built for Lansing's
150th birthday in 1997. It is at the Capitol Building.
– State Archives of Michigan

right away. The name was suggested by those settlers who came from Lansing, in Tompkins County, New York. That town was named for John Lansing, a famous man from New York.

Our Lansing is a big town now. There are 1200 people living here! Quite a change from five years ago, when only a few families lived in the area.

In 1845, we got together near our cabin for a Fourth of July party. The North and Buck families came. They live five miles away. The Cooley family lives even farther away and couldn't get here. Chief Okemos and the other Indians came, as usual, and brought their children.

The women baked bread and roasted a pig for a picnic on the river. It's almost like a park there, and all the children played tag and ran three-legged races. We had a grand time.

I've been thinking about my grandson today because it is his birthday. Marshall Pease, the first white child born in Lansing, was born the day of the picnic.

He's still too young to know how exciting it is to build a town. That's why I plan to tell him all of these stories – when he gets a little older.

1845 = 88 people in all of Lansing Township
1997 = 300,000 people in Greater Lansing

6

Will Meets the Chief

The loud barnyard rooster told Will it was time to get up. Will stretched his arms and legs, and the straw tick crackled beneath him. He remembered that Pa would be home from Dexter today. Pa had taken wheat to be ground into flour at the mill. He would trade some of the wheat for salt, coffee, and a new pair of boots at the big general store.

> A straw tick was a mattress. A large, sturdy cloth sack was stuffed with straw, and laid upon a bed frame made from logs.

After Will pulled on his shirt and pants, he climbed down the ladder to the main floor of the cabin.

His mother was making biscuits. She spooned batter into the black cast iron spider, which sat in the fireplace.

Before they had ovens, settlers cooked in kettles hung from a pole in the fireplace, or with a three-legged spider like this one.
– From Michigan State University Museum

"Good morning, Will," she said with a smile. "Ready for a busy day?"

"Yes, Ma," Will answered. He picked up a basket and went out to feed the chickens.

Will stopped at the outhouse on the way. The outhouse was their bathroom, and it stood about 50 feet behind the cabin.

> A pioneer bathroom was made by digging a deep hole and building a small shed around it for privacy. Inside, they built a box seat to go over the hole. Can you guess why it was so far from the cabin?

The chickens had a nesting house inside a small fenced yard. Will scattered corn around, and the birds scurried to their breakfast. One chicken ran between his legs and over his bare foot. "Ouch!" Will yelled. "Watch where you're going, silly bird!"

Will checked the nesting boxes. Each box had one or two eggs, and he put them carefully into the basket. Then he hurried back to the cabin.

As he walked through the door, Will stopped and gasped. Standing near his mother was a strange man. He wore a blanket coat, with a belt around the waist. Tucked into the belt was a tomahawk and a large hunting knife.

Small pipe tomahawk, used for ceremonies
— From Michigan State University Museum

His head was wrapped with a long piece of cloth, and he wore leggings and leather moccasins. Will thought he looked very old and serious.

The stranger took a loaf of bread that Will's mother held out. Then he walked over to the table, and put six steaming biscuits into his pockets. He turned and looked

Chief Okemos, late in his life
– State Archives of Michigan

at Will, then moved toward him.

Will stepped away from the door, nearly tripping over his own feet. The stranger paused, then left.

Cautiously, Will looked outside. The stranger was nowhere to be seen. "Who was he, Ma?"

"Chief Okemos," Ma said. "His people must be camped nearby. I had just put the biscuits on the table, and when I turned around he was standing there. I didn't even hear him come in."

"Do you think –" Will stopped, and looked toward the woods again. "Do you think he'll come back?" he asked in a quiet voice.

"I don't know," said Ma. "But I'm sure he doesn't mean any harm. He just wanted some food."

Then Ma pointed at the egg basket Will was holding. "Well, I better mix up a new batch of biscuits to go with those eggs!"

Will looked up at his mother and handed her the basket. "We'll be fine," she said gently. Will nodded, and felt a little better.

That afternoon, Will decided to go fishing. He walked through the woods, still thinking about the Chief. When he got close to the river, he heard splashing.

Will crouched and peeked through the trees. Two Indian boys stood in the river. Each one held a long, sharp stick.

Will watched the boys jab the water with the sticks. When they lifted them, wiggling fish were stuck on the ends. Will wanted to see them do it again, but one of the boys spotted him.

The boy nudged his companion, and pointed at Will's hiding place. Will wanted to run, but he was curious, too.

The first boy made a friendly motion with his hand, as if asking Will to come out. "*Nikaniss,*" the boy said. "*Nikaniss* – friend?"

Slowly, Will stood up and walked toward them. The three studied each other, then one of the boys pointed at Will's fishing pole.

"*Gigo?*" he asked. Will looked puzzled. "*Gigo,*" the boy said again, and he held up the fish he had speared.

"Oh – fish!" said Will. "Yes! Do you want me to show you?" he asked as they admired his pole.

The boys grinned and Will hurried with them to the river bank. They called the river "*sibi.*" Will showed his new friends how to use a fishing pole, and they showed him how to use a spear. When Will jabbed at a fish, he slipped and almost fell into the *sibi.*

Will liked fishing with his new friends. When they had caught enough for everyone, they said goodbye.

"See you later!" Will said.

"*Baa-ma!*" they answered.

Ma fixed a fine supper of *gigo,* cornbread, and carrots. Pa was home from Dexter, and they had much to talk about.

As they finished eating, the cabin door swung open and the Chief walked in. The family was surprised. Before anyone could speak, he walked over to the table and placed a large rabbit upon it.

"O-ge-mons hunt, bring meat. Give thanks," the Chief said. Then he spoke to Will. "Me teach you hunt and fish like Indian."

> The Chief's name was pronounced a little differently by the Indians and the settlers. It means "little chief." Even though he was a fierce warrior, Okemos was not a large man.

Will thought about the fishing lesson he had that day. Did the Chief know? Will looked at his Pa for approval. Then Okemos spoke again, to Pa. "Me trade you pony for boy."

Ma's eyes grew wide with surprise. "No!" she nearly shouted. Okemos frowned. Ma stood up quickly. "I mean, no – THANK you." She looked at Pa for help.

Pa stood. "You honor us, Chief. But he is our son. He is not for trade."

The Chief did not speak right away. Will looked from his Pa to his Ma, then at the Chief. Okemos patted Will on the shoulder. "Not this time," he said. "Me go now."

They heard him chuckle as he walked out.

> The Chief probably did not mean to keep Will forever. The settlers often misunderstood things the Indians said to them. He may have wanted Will to come and work for him for a few weeks, and he would teach Will useful skills. To offer a pony in "trade" was very generous.

7

Howls and Growls

The Dangerous Pet

From Mason comes a story that
  my Grandpa often told,
Of William Webb and his pet bear cub.
  Will was eight years old.
Two neighbors found a bear and three cubs
  in the woods one day.
They captured two, while mother and
  the other ran away.

They sold one to Will's father,
  for keeping as a pet.
He was the cutest little black bear
  cub you ever met.
Will chained him to a tall post in
  the yard to keep him home,
So round and
  round and
round the post
  the little cub
would roam.

– Michigan
Department of
Natural Resources,
Wildlife Division

He wound himself up one way,
  then back around he curled.
Sometimes he climbed the post and sat
  on top to see the world.
The cub was very strong, and often
  he and Will played tough.
Will would grab him with two hands
  and shake him sort of rough.

There was a problem with the neighbor
  kids, the story goes.
When the kids would get too close,
  the bear would tear their clothes.
Will's father had to sell him 'cause the
  folks were so upset,
And William Webb learned wild creatures
  never should be pets.

> Michigan has about 13,000 black bears! Most of them live in the Upper Peninsula. Some Lower Peninsula counties where black bears can be found today include Alcona, Gladwin, and Newaygo.

Dinnertime

Henry and Almira North
  were owners of a hog.
They built a pen to keep it safe,
  and covered it with logs.
They lived in Delhi Township, eighteen
  thirty-nine or so,
And worked together every day,
  to make their new farm grow.

One spring day Almira heard
  the frightened piggy squeal!
She ran outside and saw a bear,

— Michigan
Department of
Natural Resources,
Wildlife Division

the hog about to steal.
The bear pushed off the logs and tried
   to lift his dinner out.
Her husband wasn't home, so
   brave Almira gave a shout!

The bear was not afraid of her,
   he wouldn't leave his prey,
'Til Henry's brothers came with clubs
   and drove the brute away.
The hog was saved, but those big claws
   had torn his back a bit.
They stitched him up, and built a stronger
   pen because of it.

In recent years, bears have been sighted in DeWitt, Pontiac and Mt. Pleasant, but no large groups of bears are known to live there. How far are these places from your town?

The Chase

The first white man in Okemos
   was Mr. Sanford Marsh.
He had a wife, but life in eighteen
   thirty-nine was harsh.
Two years later, Bray and Barnes
   became the Marshes' neighbors.

They shared each other's friendship, and
   they shared each other's labors.

To the Marsh home, just one mile,
   Mrs. Barnes was walking.
The ladies planned to sew awhile,
   and to do some talking.
Almost there, she noticed several
   wolves were keeping pace.
She held her skirts, and on that stumpy
   trail she did race!

The wolves were swift,
   but all the time
   stayed hidden in the grass.
Mrs. Barnes looked up, and saw
   the cabin there at last!
She reached the door and
   all was safe,
   not as she had feared.
She looked back to the
   woods and saw –
   the wolves had
   disappeared.

– Michigan Department of Natural
Resources, Wildlife Division

Night Songs

In 1837, several
   cows went off to play.
The owner, Ephraim Meech, did not
   expect his cows to stray.
He searched and searched the forest wide

until it grew quite late.
When darkness came he knew that going
    home would have to wait.

Back home, his dear wife Nancy and
    their daughter went to bed.
The girl was eight, and wore a ruffled
    nightcap on her head.
The night was very quiet, save
    the whoo-whoo of an owl.
When in the distant wilderness,
    some wolves began to howl.

Closer came the animals, and
    louder came the sound.
Nancy worried that her broken
    window would be found.
She quickly built a fire so
    the wolves might be afraid.
Then spread a quilt up in the loft,
    and that is where they stayed.

Nancy and her little girl
    did not sleep well that night.
The wolves kept up their
    howling song
    until the morning light.
But when the sun at last
    came up,
    those wolves just went away
Into the forest, of a place
    called Webberville today.

When people began settling Michigan, wolves lived everywhere. In 1837, a law was made to encourage people to kill wolves. Hunters were paid $10.00 "bounty" money for each wolf shot.

Today, the gray wolf is an endangered species. In 1998, there were just 140 wolves living in the state, scattered across the Upper Peninsula.

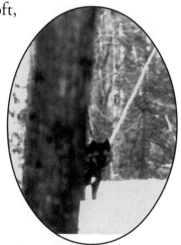

– Michigan Department of Natural Resources, Wildlife Division

8

One Cent Per Horse Per Mile

George Proctor heard the clatter of the horses and stage coach on the new plank road and ran to the door of the toll house.

George loved to visit his uncle Alonzo. It was so exciting. He had been coming from Stockbridge to visit each summer for three years, ever since he was six.

Proctor Toll House
The Toll House stood at Grand River Avenue, near Park Lake Road. It is now in Meridian Historic Village.

"I see them!" George shouted. "Can I collect the money myself?"

"That would be fine," Uncle Alonzo said. "Remember that it's one cent per horse per mile. How many horses are coming in?"

"Four," George sang out. "It's the big stage coach."

The Proctor Toll House was Gate #2 on the Lansing-to-Howell Plank Road. George knew it was five miles from the first gate in Lansing's Lower Town to their gate in Meridian Township.

How much did George collect?

Mr. Turner, Mr. Smith, and Mr. Seymour had invested their money in the new plank road. They set up a company to buy the land and materials and pay the workers to build it.

George had watched the whole thing. He was amazed when the workers set posts, fastened down two logs like runners on a sled, then placed flat hewn planks across them. They nailed the planks down with wooden pegs, and suddenly there was a section of wooden road!

> A section of the plank road was uncovered in 1995 on Grand River Avenue in East Lansing.

The workers repeated building these "sleds" until they had a road from Lansing to Howell, a total of 40 miles.

Another company had opened a plank road in 1850 from Howell to Detroit. Now people could take the stage all the way from Lansing to Detroit on the plank road. The whole trip took only 24 hours each way!

> How far could you travel in 24 hours by airplane today?

Uncle Alonzo told him the plank road was built on an old Indian trail, the Grand River Trail. The Indians walked this long, long trail from Lake Michigan to Lake Erie. It passed through Lansing and Detroit – before they were even called Lansing and Detroit.

"What did they do when they came to a river?" George asked, curious.

"Well," his uncle said, "they made sure their trails went to a low spot in the river where they could walk across. Rocky places, rapids."

When the settlers first came, they made the Indian trails wide enough for their wagons. In the swampy parts,

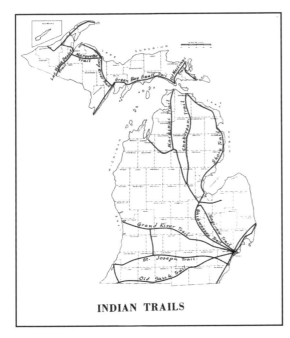

INDIAN TRAILS

Indian Trails of Michigan
Most of the major highways in Michigan follow old Indian trails. What highways replaced these Indian trails?
– Michigan Historical Commission, 1959

they threw down whole logs side by side across the muck and tied them together. These were called corduroy roads, and to George it felt like riding over giant corduroy pants.

Sometimes the passengers had to get out and help push, and sometimes the horses got their hooves caught between the logs. It took five or six days to get to Detroit then. The new plank road was so much better.

George heard the driver, Jack Stapleton, blow into his tin horn to announce his arrival. Jack called out, "Whoa, boys," and the big bay horses danced and snorted as they stopped at the Proctor gate. They were so beautiful.

And the stage coach! The metal braces on the big wooden wheels flashed in the sun, and Jack sat up high on the driver's seat all by himself. The luggage was in a trunk on the back of the stage, and the mail was in the boot under Jack's feet.

This stage coach was big enough to carry eight

TYPICAL STAGE COACH OF 1844.

Stage coach, 1844
The stage coaches delivered the mail at post office stops along the route.
People had to pay 25 cents to get a letter out of the post office. It might
be a month before they had enough cash.
– State Archives of Michigan

passengers inside on the three seats. Two people sat at the front, two at the back, and four more on a wide bench in the middle, back-to-back. Sometimes they crowded small children in, too, but today there were only six passengers.

George wanted to be a driver when he got older. He had heard about Lewis Stanton, who was already a driver and was only 16.

Lewis Stanton drove the stage coach from Lansing south to Marshall. The trip took only one day each way, even though Lewis stopped at Charlotte, Eaton Rapids, and Olivet on the way. Uncle Alonzo said that was an old Indian trail, too.

George reached up to Jack to get the money for the toll. Part of it was for Uncle Alonzo, because he was in charge of the toll house.

The rest of it was for the plank road company. The

company used the money to pay off their investment, make repairs to the road – and make a profit.

> Some states, such as Indiana and Ohio, still have toll roads. Why? Michigan has no toll roads now, but collects a toll at some bridges. Why?

George lifted the gate and waved goodbye to Jack. He knew the stage had left Lower Town at 6:00 a.m. By noon they would stop in Williamston to eat and change horses. By 6:00 p.m., they would be in Howell!

Some passengers would eat supper quickly and catch the overnight stage for Detroit, 12 more hours away.

Someday, George promised himself, he would be a driver, and he would drive all the way to Detroit. He wondered if anything could ever be faster than a stage coach with four horses.

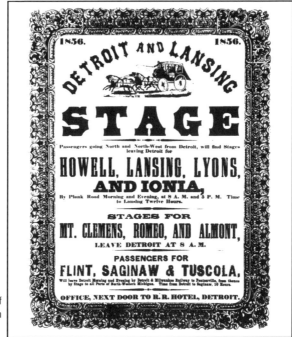

– State Archives of Michigan

9

Jennie Chapin's First Day

Jennie was a little nervous about her first day at the new school. Would the teacher be nice? Would she make any friends?

Her family had moved to Vevay Township a few weeks ago. Neighbors had told them about the school on Mr. Bristol's land, and father showed her the trail to follow through the forest.

The November air was crisp, and there was snow on the ground as Jennie walked along. The trees were bare, and the forest was quiet and gloomy. Finally, the school came into sight. It was pink, like a cherry blossom, and looking at it made her smile. Children were arriving from

The Pink School, Mason Built in 1854, the first class of 37 students ranged in age from four to fourteen.

all directions. Some walked, and others climbed out of farm wagons. Then Jennie saw a woman standing in the doorway, ringing the bell.

> Some schools had bells on the roof, in a small "cupola." A rope tied to the bell came down through a hole in the ceiling. When it was pulled, the bell rang as it tipped back and forth.

The woman wore a long brown skirt, and her cream colored blouse had ruffles at the collar and wrists. Her brown hair was swept up and fastened with silver combs. She was very pretty. Jennie went up the steps.

"Good morning! You must be Jennie," the woman said with a friendly smile. "I'm your teacher, Miss Rowe."

"Good morning, Ma'am," Jennie said.

"Well, Jennie, fourth and fifth graders sit near the middle of the classroom," Miss Rowe explained. "School will start in just a few minutes."

Jennie went inside and looked at the big, open room. There were rows of benches made from split logs, with no backs. In the middle of the room was a wood-burning stove. In the front was a very large book, laid open on a wooden stand.

> Can you guess what the book was?

Wood stove
Teachers often paid older boys to chop wood and keep the fire going during school.
– From Meridian Historic Village

Jennie hung up her coat and hat on one of the wooden pegs which lined the back wall. She sat on a bench near the warm stove, and turned to watch the other children as they came inside.

Some of the boys looked awfully big, and they pushed

each other through the door. Jennie wondered how Miss Rowe would manage them.

"Please sit down, children," Miss Rowe said, as she walked to the front of the room. "Before we start, I want you to welcome our new student, Jennie Chapin." She motioned for Jennie to stand.

From the back of the room Jennie heard a boy's voice. "Jennie, Jennie, like a new penny," the voice chanted. She sat down, looking at her shoes.

"Casper Scarlett!" Miss Rowe called angrily. "Apologize at once!"

"Aw, I'm sorry," Casper mumbled. Jennie glanced up at Miss Rowe, who smiled at her.

"Now," said Miss Rowe, "we shall work on our reading until recess, and then we shall begin the spelling bee."

Jennie was called to the front with several other children, and Miss Rowe gave them each a reader. She helped them read a few pages, and they returned to their benches to practice. While other groups were called, the rest of the children quietly worked.

When it was time for recess, they went outside to play in the snow. Jennie met a nice girl named Lucy Hawkins. They made snow angels and played fox and geese with some other boys and girls.

Jennie was having fun until Casper Scarlett ran through the circle, kicking up snow at everyone. Then Jennie saw him standing near the woodpile, whispering to another older boy. "What is he up to now?" she

Fox and Geese was a game of snow tag, played on lines made in a pie shape.

wondered. When Miss Rowe rang the bell, the children returned to their seats.

"It is time to start the spelling bee," Miss Rowe announced. "Please stand when I call your name, and do the very best you can."

Jennie listened carefully as students were called upon to spell. Older students were given bigger words than the younger ones. Miss Rowe kept track of mistakes in a notebook. Jennie waited anxiously for each turn. She had not missed yet.

> How is your school like the Pink School? How is it different?

"Jennie, please spell 'harness'."

Jennie was relieved. She knew she could do it. "Harness," she began. "H--A--R--N--E--S--S." Miss Rowe smiled and nodded. Jennie smiled brightly and began to sit down.

Just then, the girl sitting next to Jennie jumped up and screamed, "Aaagh! A mouse!"

Jennie turned and saw a little brown mouse running across the bench. She had nearly sat on it! The mouse jumped off and scurried around, as the children squealed with excitement. Finally, the frightened little creature ran into a hole in the corner. Loud laughter came from the back of the room.

"It was Casper!" Lucy shouted. "He put the mouse on her bench!" Miss Rowe hurried past the rows of children, with a hickory stick in one hand. Casper rocked back and forth on his bench with laughter. Miss Rowe grabbed his shirt at the shoulder and pulled him outside.

They were gone for several minutes, and the children inside the school were silent. When Miss Rowe returned, her face was red. She smoothed her hair and walked quietly to the front of the room.

"Very good, Jennie," said Miss Rowe. "You're the winner for today." She looked at a small watch pinned to her blouse. "It is time for lunch."

As she and Lucy ate lunch, Jennie hoped the afternoon would go quickly. She couldn't wait to tell her folks all about the new school.

Is there an old rural school near you? Look carefully – today, some of them are used as homes!

The settlers felt that education was very important, and schools were started quickly. People who taught or attended one-room schools say that in many ways it was better than today. Older kids helped younger kids, and everyone learned more by hearing the lessons repeated year after year.

10

The California Widow

In 1857, Elijah Potter decided to join a group of men who were going to California to look for gold. Gold had been discovered there in 1849. Over the years, lots of men left their homes and families to make the long journey, hoping to strike it rich.

Elijah lived with his wife, Abigail, in a large log home in Bunkerhill Township. Abigail made their home beautiful by planting pink rose bushes all around it. Elijah planted crops. They had three children, and life was good. But now Elijah was going away.

> Some gold seekers traveled by ship, and some took oxen and wagons across the plains in big caravans. It was a dangerous journey, and took up to six months. Families were left behind, not knowing if the men would ever return.

Elijah and his friends walked to Jackson, then rode a train to New York City. From there, they took a ship all the way around South America. At the Straits of Magellan, giant iceburgs endangered the small ship. They finally made it around Cape Horn, and up to California one month later. They began their search in San Francisco.

Elijah spent five years looking for gold in many towns. He found a little, but in letters home he complained that the best time for gold strikes had passed. One good thing did happen – his health improved.

Like many Michigan pioneers, Elijah had suffered from ague since he was a child. In California, he gained

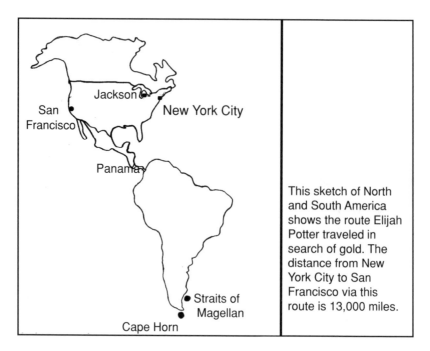

This sketch of North and South America shows the route Elijah Potter traveled in search of gold. The distance from New York City to San Francisco via this route is 13,000 miles.

weight and felt much better. In his letters, he also gave Abigail lots of advice on how to run the farm.

> The sweating, fever, and uncontrollable shakes of ague could come and go for years.

Abigail did not pay attention to Elijah's advice. She was very independent, and had her own ideas. In letters that Abigail wrote during this time, she called herself a "California widow." She had lost her husband to California. But she had spunk and determination, and she knew she could keep the farm going.

She got some help from Elijah's brothers during planting and harvesting time, and she also hired some help. But Abigail was in charge. She made all the decisions. She took good care of the money that she made from selling crops. The farm prospered.

In 1862, Elijah gave up on the gold and began the long trip home. He reserved a spot on a ship called the

"Golden Gate." Somehow, on the morning the ship departed, Elijah slept too long and missed it! This turned out to be very lucky. He heard later that the ship had caught fire and burned.

Elijah found another ship, but he did not plan to go through the Straits of Magellan again. When the ship got to Panama, Elijah got off. He walked fifty miles across the isthmus through hot, tropical jungles.

> The Isthmus of Panama is a narrow strip of land connecting North and South America.

When he reached the other side, Elijah took a ship to New York. Then he rode a train back to Jackson, Michigan. He got there on February 10, 1863, and began to walk north toward his home.

Elijah Potter, 1857
Photo taken in New York, when Elijah was on his way to California.
– John Curry

Abigail Potter, c. 1860
– John Curry

Back at home, Abigail had been told that her husband was on a list of missing people from the "Golden Gate" fire. Elijah was thought to be dead. Abigail planned a memorial service for him in the Methodist Church on February 10th.

Elijah arrived that afternoon, and saw a crowd of people at the church. He was curious, so he slipped quietly inside and stood at the back of the room. He soon realized that he was attending his own funeral! Everyone was amazed that Elijah was alive, and people talked about that day for many years.

Elijah and Abigail kept on farming, and had three more children. Elijah bought more land, and managed their growing farm. In time, they owned 600 acres.

Elijah became one of the wealthiest men in Ingham county, not because of the gold he left home for, but because of the farm which his good wife held together.

Grettenberger farm house at Meridian Historic Village
By 1860, Greek Revival houses were popular
on the farms and in towns.

11

Awfully Long and Terribly Bumpy

It seemed to Jimmy Turner that every town had trains before Lansing did.

Jackson got a railroad from Detroit in 1841. By 1852, those tracks went through Marshall and Battle Creek and all the way to Chicago. Jackson got another railroad, from Toledo, in 1857. Jimmy was only seven then!

In 1862, the tracks finally reached the northeast corner of Lansing, from Owosso. The train stood at the new station at the Ballard farm on Franklin Street. "AL&TB" was painted on the cab of the engine. It was very big, and very noisy.

Lansing's First Train
The tracks reached Michigan Avenue in 1863
– Local History Room, Lansing Library

Banners that read "Amboy, Lansing and Traverse Bay RR" flapped in the wind. A band played, men made speeches, and a lot of people came to ride on the train. Jimmy planned to be first in line.

At the clang of the bell and the "All-l-l abo-o-o-ard," he ran to find a seat. When he heard the *chugga, chugga, chugga* of the steam engine, he was speechless.

Finally, the steam whooshed out from under the engine, and the train lurched out of the station. The passengers held on tight to their seats. They were off for Owosso!

Owosso was only 28 miles away, but the trip would take almost three hours.

After a while, Jimmy heard a loud woman complaining. "This ticket costs $1.25, each way!" she said. "That's the same as the stage coach, and this is so bumpy."

"Why are you taking the train then?" a little girl said.

"Oh, I'm not paying," the woman said. "I get to ride free."

The little girl looked puzzled. The woman puffed herself up. "I get to ride free for one year," she said. "It's part of my 'arrangement' with the railroad company. I sold them some land to lay the tracks on."

She pulled her knitting out of her bag. "I'll be riding again next week, you know." She clucked her tongue. "I certainly do hope we make it to Owosso in time to catch the train to Detroit."

Jimmy ducked his head and smiled. Little Orlando Barnes slid into the seat beside him.

"Did you see what those people are doing?" Jimmy said. He pointed at some people walking near the train. "They are picking berries. Wanna get off and pick some?"

"Off the train?" Orlando said. "We'd get stuck out here."

"Naw," Jimmy said. "The train is so slow you can just run a little and get back on. See? Here they come."

The train bumped along a little faster, and it was too late to get off.

Out the corner of his eye, Jimmy could see their fathers, talking with some other men. Jimmy poked Orlando with his elbow. "Look at my father," he said. "His bow tie moves whenever he talks."

Orlando started to get on his knees so he could see over the seat. Jimmy grabbed him. "Don't turn *around* and look! Peek between the seats."

"Just like the plank roads," big Jim Turner was saying. "You have to form a company. Invest your money. Buy land from the farmers. Lay the tracks. Buy the train."

His bow tie bobbed with each statement. The boys tried not to laugh out loud.

"Why should I put up that much money?" a man said. "That's crazy. Why would Lansing want two railroads?"

James Turner
Investor in Lansing-to-Howell Plank Road Company and Michigan Female College, Deputy State Treasurer, and Senator.
— Local History Room, Lansing Library

"Jackson has two," Mr. Barnes said, "and two more planned." He noticed his son peeking between the seats, but didn't say anything to him. "We want to make Lansing an important center for trains, too."

"We need 'em if we're going to grow," Jim Turner said. "Grain. Passengers." The bow tie bobbed in time to the words. "Faster. People always want to get some place faster."

The second railroad, the Jackson, Lansing & Saginaw RR, came to Lansing in 1866. Later, the train went on past Saginaw all the way to Mackinaw City – 290 miles. Mr. Turner and Mr. Barnes were part of this company.

"There's a good deal of money to be made," Mr. Barnes said. "Ask Mr. Case here what they did in Jackson. They invested because they could see the future."

Jimmy and Orlando lost interest, even in the bow tie. It seemed like a long, long way to Owosso.

The train made a huge lurch again, and Jimmy nudged Orlando.

"You know what they should call this train? Not the Amboy, Lansing & Traverse Bay. They should call it the <u>A</u>wfully <u>L</u>ong and <u>T</u>erribly <u>B</u>umpy!"

The Barnes Family
Mariette, Orlando M., Orlando F., Amanda, Edward
Orlando M. Barnes was an attorney, Ingham County Prosecutor, Mayor of Lansing, and investor in many businesses.
— Phil Siebert

Orlando F. Barnes (little Orlando), became an investor in several businesses.

James M. Turner (Jimmy), became a State Representative, Mayor of Lansing, and an investor in railroads and a milk company.

12

Anna and the Civil War

Like most girls, Anna Ballard went to school, learned to spin and sew, worked in the garden, and played with her brothers and sisters on their farm. When she was twelve years old, *four* of her brothers went off to the Civil War.

The Civil War started in 1861, and President Lincoln called for men from all of the Northern states to volunteer for an army.

The very next day, Governor Blair and Senator Zach Chandler began to hold rallys to find soldiers. They went to town halls and country schools and persuaded young men to sign up to fight in the war.

> People in the South wanted to be a separate country and keep their slaves. People in the North wanted to stay as one country and free the slaves. The North won the war.

They held the first rally at the Capitol Building. Seymour Foster, a friend of Anna's, was too young to get into the meeting. He had to wait outside. He told her he climbed up the side of the capitol and looked in the window.

The hall was packed with young men; the speeches were exciting. When the governor thundered, "Who will serve?" Seymour watched his older brother work his way to the front of the room. Charles Foster was the first young man from Lansing to volunteer for the war.

James Ballard, Anna's oldest brother, signed the papers, too. And then Henry, her next brother, signed up.

Even Alonzo, who was only 17, signed a few days later. Anna's fourth brother lived in Kansas, and he signed up there.

> Both Foster and James Ballard were in the First Michigan Volunteer Infantry. About 90,000 men from Michigan fought in the Civil War, including many "negroes."

Both Alonzo and Henry Ballard joined the U.S. Sharpshooters. To be chosen, they had to shoot ten bullets in a row into a small round target, from two hundred yards away. They said it was like hunting rabbits. Soon, they were in battles in the South.

After the trains reached Lansing in 1862, Anna watched hundreds of soldiers leave for the war from the station at their farm. She thought they were so brave.

First Michigan Sharpshooters, Capitol Lawn
— Rod Cranson

The U. S. Sharpshooters were famous among the soldiers on both sides of the war. They fought in every major battle in Virginia, and at Gettysburg.

Then word came that Charles Foster had been killed. He was carrying the flag for his company when he was shot. His mother received a letter he wrote before he died. He told her he would carry the flag because it was a great honor, and no one else volunteered: it was so dangerous.

Anna cried and wondered why anyone went to war at all. But Alonzo wrote to her and said men needed to fight for what they believed in. They couldn't let the country be torn apart.

Alonzo wrote other letters home, telling about the soldiers' daily life. In one letter, he wrote, "While on the march we [ate] nothing but pork hardbread coffee and sugar."

To his younger brother he wrote, "It rains most of the time and is so muddy we can't hardly get around. . . . Tell me all about your evening visits with the young ladies."

Three Ballard Sisters, 1862
Alonzo carried this photo during the Civil War.
—Suzanne Ballard Sell

In other letters, Alonzo wrote about the fevers the soldiers always had. Many soldiers got the measles, too. A friend of Alonzo's wrote to him: "I suppose you recollect well . . . when we reached the White House . . . I was so sick when I layed down that I could have went to sleep in a mud hole."

Sickness and disease took the lives of more soldiers than the battles did. Anna read these letters and

> Most cemeteries have a special Civil War section, where the soldiers are buried.

Anna and Alonzo Ballard
— Suzanne Ballard Sell

wondered if there was anything she could do.

After the war ended in 1865, Alonzo decided to go to Kansas with his brother, David. James had died in Virginia. Henry came home, wounded.

Anna was sixteen. She was a student at the Michigan Female College in Lansing. The teachers told the girls to be strong thinkers, and to think about what they believed in.

The girls all knew about Miss Augusta Chapin, who taught at the College when Anna's older sister went there. Miss Chapin knew that she wanted to be a minister. In 1863, she was the first woman in Michigan to be ordained. She was already quite famous.

The girls also knew about the woman from Lansing who fought in the Civil War. She dressed up as a man, and nobody found out! Like Anna's brother, she believed in *fighting* for what she believed in.

The girls learned about some women in New York who believed that women should be able to vote. Anna liked that idea, but she kept looking for her own belief.

> The first meeting of the Women's Suffrage Movement (the right to vote) was held at Seneca Falls, New York, in 1848; 300 women attended.

Before long, Anna went to work for her brother-in-law, Dr. Topping, in his drug store in DeWitt. She liked the work, and she began to have an idea of what she believed in. Anna asked Dr. Topping to teach her about medicine.

A few years later, Anna Ballard decided to become a doctor. She took a course in medicine at the University of Michigan, and then went to medical school in Chicago.

In 1879, Dr. Anna Ballard came back to Lansing to practice medicine. She was the first woman doctor in town. She believed in medicine until her death, 55 years later.

Dr. Anna Ballard
— Suzanne Ballard Sell

13

The Great Detective Story

"Look at this!" Luther Baker shouted to his sister. He waved a telegram in the air. "Lafayette wants me to come to Washington D.C.! He wants me to work with him!"

Their cousin, General Lafayette C. Baker, was head of the "Detective Bureau" for the United States. The Civil War was raging, and he needed more detectives.

Luther liked the idea of being a detective. It sounded more exciting than working in the bookstore. Maybe he would track down bank robbers. Maybe he could be a spy!

Luther soon became a lieutenant in the First District of Columbia Cavalry, a unit of secret service agents. They were important spies for the North during the Civil War.

General Lafayette C. Baker
– History of the Secret Service
1867

Just after the war was over, a terrible thing happened. On April 14, 1865, a man shot and killed the president of the United States, Abraham Lincoln.

President and Mrs. Lincoln had gone to see a play

at Ford's Theater. During the play, people in the theater heard gunfire. Someone cried out, "The president has been shot!" The people screamed and rushed out the front doors of the theater.

The man who shot the president jumped to the stage from the president's box and ran out the back door. He escaped on a horse which his friends had put outside the theater for him.

The men in the Detective Service were asked to find the gunman. Among them was Lieutenant Luther Baker.

The assassin was John Wilkes Booth, a famous actor and speaker. Booth and his friends had favored the South in the Civil War, and Booth made many speeches against President Lincoln. A month before, Booth and his friends

Luther Baker on Buckskin; President Abraham Lincoln; John Wilkes Booth
– Michigan State University Museum

failed in a scheme to kidnap the president. This new scheme, to kill the president, worked.

When Booth jumped down to the stage, he broke his leg very badly. Within a few hours, he was in great pain and needed a doctor.

He found the office of Dr. Mudd, who had not yet heard about the shooting. The doctor put a splint on his leg, and Booth rode off again.

> Many people have said that Dr. Mudd should not have treated Booth's leg, because he killed the President. What do you think?

> The expression "Your name is mud" comes from this event.

Many people were looking for Booth, and many were sure that Booth was hiding near Washington D.C. Not General Baker. General Baker felt that Booth would try to go south to stay with friends who would hide him. He put Lieutenant Luther Baker in charge of a team of detectives to go hunt for him.

The detectives crossed the Potomac River into Virginia. The second day, Luther Baker found a fisherman who had taken a lame man across the Rappahannock River. Luther was thrilled that he had "struck the trail."

The detectives tracked down one of Booth's friends and forced him to reveal Booth's hiding place. The man led them to a farm a few miles away. The farmer's son admitted that Booth was hiding in their barn and that Booth had guns.

The detectives took their places around the barn, weapons ready. Luther Baker went to the door of the barn. "Booth, put down your guns," he commanded. "Come out!"

"Who are you?" Booth shouted back.

"It doesn't matter," Baker said. "We know who you

are. Come out and surrender."

When there was no answer, Baker said, "Come out in two minutes or we'll set the barn on fire."

Booth did not come out, and the detectives set the barn on fire. The detectives, looking through the cracks in the side of the barn, could see the fire leap all around Booth.

Booth was holding two guns, and many of the men feared he would shoot Luther Baker if he came out. Just as Booth started to move, one of the detectives shot him.

The detectives pulled Booth out of the barn, and Luther Baker held him while he died. Booth asked Baker to tell his mother that he did it for his country. His dying words were, "Useless, useless . . . ."

Both General Lafayette Baker and Lieutenant Luther Baker were given rewards for finding the assassin of the president. Some say Luther's reward was as much as

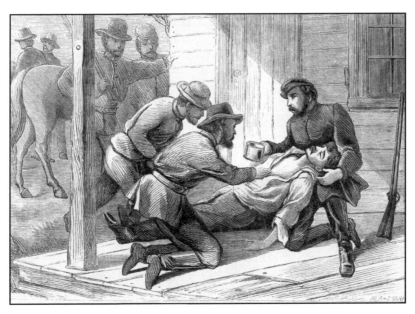

Lieutenant Luther Baker holding the dying John Wilkes Booth.
– History of the Secret Service, 1867

$5,000.00. He looked around for something to do with the money.

General Baker had grown up near Lansing, the large capital city of

How much is $5,000.00 today? If you had that much money today, what would you do with it?

Michigan. His father and mother told their nephew Luther that Lansing needed a good hotel. The legislators and visitors needed a nice place to stay while they were in town.

Lieutenant Luther Baker moved to Lansing, went to work for the State of Michigan, and invested his reward money in the new Lansing House Hotel.

Baker married Helen Davis, the daughter of a pioneer family in Lansing. Her parents had a large farm south of town.

The Lansing House (Downey) Hotel
– Local History Room, Lansing Library

For the rest of his life, Luther Baker was called a hero. For many years, he gave talks about the capture of John Wilkes Booth and led all of the parades in Lansing. In the parades, he rode his famous horse, Buckskin, the horse he had ridden during the capture of John Wilkes Booth.

Baker Street in Lansing is named for Luther Baker. It's between S. Cedar and S. Washington, and between the railroad tracks and Mt. Hope. This was the location of the Davis farm, where Luther and Helen Baker later lived.

When Buckskin died, he was stuffed and put on display at the Michigan State University Museum. After many years, parts were falling off and Buckskin was put in storage.

ASSASSINATION
ᴏꜰ
Abraham Lincoln
THE PURSUIT, CAPTURE, DEATH AND BURIAL OF
J.WILKESBOOTH,
HIS ASSASSIN.

LECTURE
—BY—
LIEUT. L. B. BAKER,
OF LANSING, MICH.

AT OPERA HALL.
THURSDAY EVENING, MARCH 19, 1891.
FOR THE BENEFIT OF JOHN F. REYNOLDS
POST G. A. R. OF PENTWATER, MICH.

Lieut. Baker was in command of the capturing party and is more competent to tell the story than any other living person.   Everybody come.

Admission, 20c.   Children 10c.

LIEUT. BAKER,
ASSASSINATION OF LINCOLN
—AND—
Capture and Death of Booth.
ADMIT ONE.

Poster and ticket for a speech given by Luther Baker
– Michigan State University Museum

14

The Younger Son

Darius Moon glared at his oldest brother and the wagon full of furniture. Darius jutted his chin out and crossed his arms. He was very angry, but he could not say anything.

He was already fifteen – but he was the younger son, and younger sons could not object.

Darius Moon
His first name is "Duh-RI-us"
– Woldumar Nature Center

His brother jumped up onto the wagon seat, grabbed the reins, and clucked at the horses. The horses pulled away slowly. His brother did not look back. He was headed for Iowa to settle on a new farm.

Darius noticed that his mother had tears in her eyes. "Don't worry," Darius said. "I'll take care of you." Then he turned his head away so his mother would not see how angry he was.

In his mind, Darius added up three reasons for being angry. One, his brother was taking the best horses and wagon with him. Two, his brother had sold part of their farm. And three, the most disgusting thing, his brother kept all of the money for himself.

He did not give any of the money to Darius or his mother, even though the whole family worked hard on the farm for twelve years.

Darius was only three when they came to Delta Township, west of Lansing, in 1854. Even when he was little, he helped clear the fields by picking up stones.

For the first year, three families of aunts and uncles and cousins all lived together in one log cabin. There were 27 of them.

The women cooked outside in big kettles set over a fire. The children slept in rows in the loft, lined up like sweet corn.

When Darius was eight, his family built a new log cabin. He helped hold the logs in place while the men rolled them up. He helped build pens for the cow and the hogs so the wolves could not get them. He was good with a hammer.

Moon Cabin, 1859
– Woldumar Nature Center

As the land was cleared, Darius and his brothers planted potatoes in little slits they chopped in the ground. They planted corn in little hills of dirt. They plowed the fields for wheat and hauled the heavy bags of grain to the Ingersoll mill to be ground into flour.

It took all day, every day, and it was hard, hard work.

And now, after all these years of work, Darius watched his brother drive away with their horses and money. His father was never around. Darius didn't see how they would survive.

Besides, he hated farm work. He had hoped to leave the farm himself. Now he needed to help support his mother and brothers, but what else could he do to earn money?

He knew he had to set his anger aside. He couldn't think clearly when he was angry.

He decided to take stock of what he had. He had a strong body, the ability to work hard, and a talent for "figuring." He liked to draw and build things.

The next day, he walked to a neighbor's farm and offered to hire on as a carpenter to help build their new barn. The neighbor sent him home, saying, "I can hire men with more experience who will eat a lot less than you do."

Darius was disappointed, and went back to work in the fields. But the idea of getting paid to build things grew stronger.

A few weeks later, Darius found carpenter's work farther from home. He put down his hoe and never farmed again.

At first, Darius worked for other men as an apprentice carpenter. The master carpenters trained him on the job.

The carpenters worked six days a week. They ate and slept at the job site. On Saturday nights after work, he walked to his mother's farm, spent Sunday there, and then walked back to work on Monday morning.

Carpenters' Tools
– From Michigan State University Museum

Sometimes the jobs were so far away that he had to leave home at four o'clock in the morning to get to work. As soon as he had enough money, he bought a horse.

Carpentry work is quite dangerous. One time Darius fell through a stairwell that had no stair yet. Another time, he fell off a barn roof and landed – unhurt – beside a big rock. He felt very lucky.

After a few years, he became the boss and hired his own crew of carpenters. For 20 years, he built sheds and barns and houses all over the Lansing area.

He ordered house designs and fancy brackets, lintels, and other trims from catalogs. He became well known as a carpenter.

Hungerford House, 1880

Close-up view of windows
Lintels are the trim pieces at the tops of windows.

But he wanted to be an architect. He wanted to *draw* the buildings.

In 1889, the City of Lansing held a contest for the best design for a new elementary school. Darius entered one of his designs – and he won the contest! After that, he became well known as an architect.

Over his lifetime, Darius Moon worked on about 275 projects. He is one of the most famous architects from Lansing.

Rogers House, 1891
529 N. Capitol Ave.
– Local History Room,
Lansing Library

Moon House, 1894
216 N. Huron
Queen Anne house built
for his own family. It was
rescued in the 1970s and
moved from Michigan
Avenue.
– Local History Room,
Lansing Library

R.E. Olds House, 1902 (demolished)
700 Block of S. Washington
– Local History Room, Lansing Library

Gunnisonville School, 1905
Clark Road at Wood Road
(available for school use)
– Local History Room,
Lansing Library

– 15 –

Guten Nacht

Jacob Sindlinger followed the spicy smell of molasses into the kitchen, where his mother was working. "Did you make *Lebkuchen* for the Christmas party?" Jacob asked.

"Ah, you smelled it baking. I'm almost finished," Mother said, as she spread glaze on the warm bar cookies.

"Lebkuchen" means "gingerbread."

Jacob's father came into the kitchen. "Would you please fix my tie?" he asked Mother.

"*Ja.* You both look very handsome," Mother said, as she straightened the tie.

"Ja" means "yes."

Mother covered the *Lebkuchen*. "Jacob," she said, "please carry the basket of dishes."

They walked to the Liederkranz Club on North Grand Street in Lansing. It was a special place for German people to meet each other and have fun. Once a month they had a big Sauerkraut Supper. The sauerkraut was served with pork, mashed potatoes and gravy, beans, and lots of desserts. After the supper everyone would dance to polka music and sing.

Singing was part of everyday life in Germany. Families sang together at home, at church, and when they visited other families. When groups of German immigrants settled in Michigan, they continued the tradition.

Now it was a few days before Christmas, and Jacob was looking forward to a special celebration at the club.

Jacob and his parents chose seats at a long table in the dining room, next to the Burkle family. "Hi, *Freund!*" Emanuel Burkle said when he saw Jacob. Jacob was glad to see his friend.

> *"Freund"* means "friend."

The boys watched as others came in and took seats. Jacob had just seen many of these faces at church last Sunday.

There was a German Methodist church and a German Lutheran church within walking distance of the Liederkranz club. Jacob's family went to the Lutheran church. The minister spoke the entire church service in their native language.

> Emanuel First Evangelical Lutheran Church, on Capitol Avenue, Lansing, still has one service every week in German.

Even though they knew English, it was nice to have people around to speak German with. Jacob's father said it was important not to forget. Jacob had heard about a German church in Delhi Township, too. He thought there must be a lot of German settlers in Michigan.

Down at the end of the table was Christian Ziegler, the man who started the club in 1868. Before the new clubhouse was built, he held the meetings in his home.

Liederkranz Hall
– Local History Room,
Lansing Library

Jacob noticed how full the room was now. The club had really grown in four years.

Soon the food was passed up and down the long tables, and everyone was eating. Jacob and Emanuel couldn't wait for the desserts, like apple cake with streusel topping, and the *Lebkuchen* Jacob's mother had brought.

Emanuel's mother had made *Springerle*, a very special holiday cookie. *Springerle* was made by pressing wooden molds onto rolled out dough. The molds were hand-carved with tiny Christmas scenes and borders. The lemony cookies did not taste fancy, but they were beautiful to look at. Emanuel's mother had brought her molds all the way from Germany, and only made *Springerle* at Christmas.

Springerle molds and the finished cookies
Some people use the cookies for Christmas tree ornaments.
– Andra Scott Price

After supper, the women cleared the tables and washed the dishes. The men and children moved into the meeting room to talk. Jacob admired the Christmas tree, a beautiful blue spruce. It filled a corner of the room, and almost touched the ceiling.

Apples and little shafts of wheat hung on the tree. Small candles were fastened onto the ends of its branches. One of the men began to light the candles. Jacob smiled.

It looked like little stars had come inside.

In another corner, Rosa Sutsel was reading a story to the smaller children. Soon the women joined the group, and it was time for carols.

Mr. Ziegler brought out his violin and began to play *"Ihr Kinderlein Kommet."* It sounded so nice to hear all the voices and the violin music. After they sang *"O Tannenbaum,"* the children were given little knitted stockings filled with nuts and candy.

The last song, *"Stille Nacht, Heilige Nacht,"* was Jacob's favorite. Two men put out all the candles on the tree, and the party was over.

Outside, Jacob and his parents called *"Guten Nacht!"* and "Merry Christmas!" to their friends. Up and down the street, people were singing as they walked home under softly falling snow.

"Stille Nacht, Heilige Nacht," is "Silent Night, Holy Night."
"Ihr Kinderlein Kommet," is "O Come, Little Children."
"O Tannenbaum," is "O Christmas Tree."

Stone Cutters

Look at this old photograph. A workman is sitting on a block of stone carved with a date. Men are posed behind the stone. It looks official, but a boy and two girls stand shyly at the side. Why would they be in the photo?

Let's start with that huge block of stone. It is the cornerstone for the new Capitol Building, and it weighs five tons. The date carved in the stone, 1872, shows when the building was started.

Cornerstone of Capitol
Eban McPhee, Stone Cutter
– State Archives of Michigan

The capitol was the biggest building the state had ever built. It contained 139 rooms, intricate metal chandeliers, and colored glass in the ceilings. The outside is sandstone; fifteen million bricks manufactured in Lansing were used for the inside walls. It cost $1,500,000.00 and took six years to build.

> Elijah E. Myers, the architect of the Michigan Capitol, also designed the capitols for Texas and Colorado.

Interior of Capitol
— State Archives of Michigan

For the first year, stone cutters laid the foundations for the Capitol. When the foundations were done, a ceremony was planned for the laying of the cornerstone. It would be the biggest party Michigan had ever seen.

Thirty thousand people arrived in Lansing for the celebration on October 2, 1873. They knew that such an event would never happen again in their lifetimes.

Special trains brought people from all over the state to celebrate. Hotels were full. Ladies from the churches baked chickens and cakes to sell. Hundreds of men pressed their uniforms or polished their trumpets and trombones, getting ready for the huge parade. Tattered Civil War battle flags flew from the grandstand.

Crowd at cornerstone ceremony
– State Archives of Michigan

Three days before the ceremony, the special five-ton cornerstone had arrived from Philadelphia on the train. Four horses dragged it from the train station to the Capitol. Hundreds of people followed it, especially the children in the photo.

The girls are in the photo because they are Orah and Lizzie Glaister, the daughters of the master stone mason. The boy is probably their brother, Joseph. Their father, Richard Glaister, was the superintendent of the stone work on the Capitol. He was one of the most important men on the project.

Mr. Glaister had worked on Trinity Church in Pittsburg, City Hall in Detroit, and the Parliament Buildings in Ottawa, Canada, before he moved his family to Lansing.

> James Appleyard was important, also. He was superintendent of construction for the Capitol.

Orah and Lizzie and Joseph visited the capitol grounds every day. They watched the giant wooden cranes

Yard of the Capitol, showing stacked stone and derricks, 1872
— State Archives of Michigan

and ropes hoist the three-foot thick foundation stones into place. They watched the stone cutters carefully chip the edges of the stones to make them fit together tight. The construction site rang with shouts and hammering. It was the most exciting place in town to be.

Stone Cutters, 1875
— State Archives of Michigan

79

The cornerstone came with a cavity cut into it for a time capsule. The time capsule was a 16-inch copper and glass box. It contained a history of Michigan, newspapers, and gold and silver coins. The highlight of the ceremony would be to unveil the cornerstone – and set the time capsule into the cavity.

> What would you put in a time capsule today?

Two days before the ceremony, the horses and the stone cutters dragged the stone into place. Then they decided to make sure the time capsule would fit.

It didn't fit. The hole was too small.

Immediately, Mr. Glaister told Eban McPhee, one of the stone cutters, to make the cavity bigger. And that's what he is doing in the photo. He is sitting on top of the cornerstone, chipping away some of the stone, very, very carefully. People collected the chips for souvenirs.

And a photographer told the men who were watching to move closer together, and sure, get the children in there, too, and let's get a picture of this.

Capitol, 1875
– State Archives of Michigan

Finished Capitol Building (above); Old and New Capitol Buildings (below)
— State Archives of Michigan

– 17 –

Sweet Harvest

The breath of the horses made little white clouds as they trotted through the snow. Irvin, Clair, and Elda Wilkins rode in the big sled with their father. It was early March, and the children were excited about the work that lay ahead.

They were going to the sugar bush at the back of their farm to "tap" the trees. The sap would be used to make heavenly treats, like maple syrup, sugar, cream, and even candy.

> A sugar bush is a grove of sugar maple trees from which farmers collect sap.

Most farmers made sugar. It was something to do at the end of winter, when people were tired of being inside so much. Maple sugar could be used like cash at the general store. The postmaster would also accept a small cake of sugar as payment for the mail.

Sugaring started in February or March, and lasted four to six weeks. As long as the nights were freezing and the days were warm, the sap would run. When frogs started croaking and spring flowers bloomed, the season was over.

Pa stopped the horses near the sugar house, and gave each child two wooden buckets to get started.

At the first tree, Pa drilled a small hole in the bark, at a slight upward angle. Then he gently tapped a spile into the hole with his hammer. The middle of the spile was like a tiny straw from which the sap would drip out .

Little Elda hung a bucket from a hook on the spile. She laughed as the clear liquid began to drip into the bucket, drip-drop, drip-drop. "Two drops per heartbeat – that's a good flow," said Pa.

Elda put her finger under the spile and caught one little drop. She stuck the finger into her mouth. It tasted like water,

Old spiles and sugar devil
The sugar devil was a tool used to get hardened maple sugar out of a large tub.

with just a tiny hint of sweetness.

They moved on to another tree, and Elda hung her second bucket. Then she trudged back to the sled for two more. Clair and Irvin hung their buckets next. Some of the bigger trees could hold two buckets. If a tree was skinny

enough for little Elda to put her arms around and clasp her hands, Pa said it was too young to tap. With Pa tapping, and the children going back and forth, they soon had sap from 300 trees drip-dropping into the buckets.

Inside the sugar house, a big firebox called an "arch" took up most of the room. It stood about three feet high. On top of

It takes a lot of wood to keep the fire going
Today, the Wilkins' sugar bush is part of Sugar Bush Supplies in Mason. The old sugar house is still used every year. Inside is a modern boiling pan, called an evaporator.

the arch was a very long, flat pan with sides. This is where they would boil the sap.

Wood that had been cut and stacked months before was ready to be burned in the arch. The fire would heat the pan, and when all of the extra water in the sap boiled away, sweet maple syrup would be left. Pa started the fire, and Clair was in charge of keeping it going.

At lunchtime, Pa and the children shared a basket of food Ma had packed. The children gave the horses some hay and water. Clair and Irvin filled buckets with snow, set them near the warm arch to melt, and then put them in front of the horses.

After they finished eating, Pa drove the team closer to the tapped trees. Some of the buckets were half full already. He and Irvin began emptying them into a barrel in the back of the sled.

When the barrel was full, Pa drove the team over to the sugar house, and poured the sap into a big holding tank outside. The tank stood up high, and was connected to the boiling pan by a pipe through the wall. The sap ran down into the pan, and started to simmer.

Soon, the sap began to boil. Great clouds of steam rose from the pan and floated out the cupola vents. Elda stayed in the sugar house with Clair, while Pa and Irvin collected more sap.

> It takes fourteen gallons of sap to make one quart of syrup. How many gallons of sap would it take to make one gallon of syrup? (In one day, a tree can give two or three gallons of sap.)

The sugar house was a cozy place. The sweet, woodsy smell of maple filled the air, and the fire kept them very warm.

As they watched the bubbling sap, Clair and Elda talked about the little maple candies Mother would make, and how good the syrup would taste on hot buckwheat pancakes and biscuits.

After a couple of hours, Pa opened a spout at the corner of the boiling pan. The stream of syrup ran through a funnel into a milk can. In a day or two, the sugar sand would sink to the bottom. Then Ma would pour the syrup into her big kettle in the kitchen, and finish cooking it on the stove. She would have to mix in a little milk and some eggs, and skim off the top from time to time. Then the syrup would be very pure.

Pa and Irvin kept bringing more sap to add to the tank, and it flowed into the pan and boiled down to sweet, golden syrup all afternoon.

When the last batch for the day was bubbling in the pan, the children knew they would make snow candy.

They each took a small wooden bowl and filled it with a scoop of clean snow.

Pa had cooked a pan full of syrup on a small cook-stove to make it thicker. He poured the hot, thick syrup onto each bowlful of snow. The syrup stiffened into a delicious cool treat the children ate with their fingers. It was a fine ending for a wonderful, sweet harvest.

> The Indians tapped trees and made syrup, too. They made a slash in the bark, and caught the sap in a carved out tree stump. If they did not have kettles, they boiled the sap in a hollowed out log. They put hot rocks from the fire into the sap, and kept doing this until it boiled. Imagine how long that would have taken!

Sugar camp of Chief Shoppengon near Frederic, Michigan, c. 1880
– George Fogle, Sugar Bush Supplies

– 18 –

The Buried Seeds

Jessie Beal's father was always trying to learn more about plants. He pruned the apple trees every month to see if that would help them grow. He cut some little tree trunks to use for fence posts. He set some of them right side up, and some upside down. He wanted to know if they rotted slower upside down, as some people said.

He started a flower garden. He started a grass garden. He started a weed garden. He put labels on his plants and made notes about them every day.

Dr. William James Beal was a professor of botany at Michigan Agricultural College. He tested everything he could think of about plants.

From all over the state, young men went to M.A.C. to study "scientific farming." They studied soil and

M.A.C. opened in 1857. The college is now called Michigan State University.

Dr. William J. Beal
– Michigan State University Archives

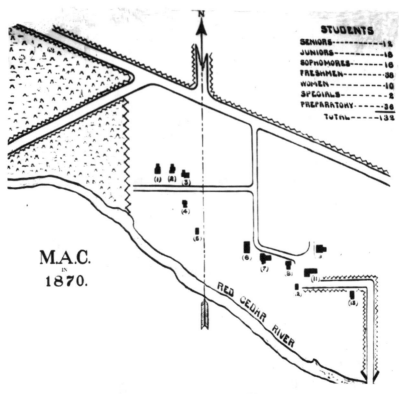

STUDENTS
SENIORS--------------12
JUNIORS-----------16
SOPHOMORES--------16
FRESHMEN----------88
WOMEN------------10
SPECIALS--------2
PREPARATORY-----36
TOTAL----132

M.A.C.
ᴵᴺ
1870.

RED CEDAR RIVER

— Michigan State University Archives

NAMES OF THE FACULTY:

T. C. ABBOT, A.M. PRESIDENT
   Prof. of Mental Philosophy and Logic
MANLY MILES, M.D.,
   Professor of Agriculture
R. C. KEDZIE, A.M. M.D.,
   Prof. of Chemistry
SANFORD HOWARD,
   Secretary
GEORGE T. FAIRCHILD, A.M.,
   Prof. of English Literature
ALBERT J. COOK, M.S.,
   Prof. of Zoology
WILL W. TRACY, B.S.,
   Instructor in Horticulture
RICHARD HAIGH, JR., B.S.,
   Asst. Secretary
WILLIAM J. BEAL, A.M., B.S.,
   Lecturer on Botany
J. J. GOLARD–FERNAND,
   Instructor in French

LEGEND–
Houses: 1) Dr. Miles
         2) Dr. Kedzie
         3) Prof. Fairchild
         4) Pres. Abbot
      5) Greenhouse
      6) College Hall
      7) Williams Hall
      8) Saints Rest
      9) Farm House
     11) Old Barn
     12) Brick Horse Barn
     13) Herdsman's House

In 1870, the college allowed women to attend.

fertilizer, trying to make the crops grow better. They also studied English, law, philosophy, and math. They went to classes in the mornings and worked on the farms in the afternoons.

Jessie's parents moved to M.A.C. in 1870, the same year she was born. The campus was a very small place for a child to grow up. There were six houses, one for each professor, and one dormitory where the students stayed. There was one classroom building, a library and office building, the laboratories where her father worked, and barns. There were not many children.

The college was out in the country, three miles east of Lansing. The road was

Linton Hall, M.A.C.
Drinking fountain for people on the front, and horses on the back.
– Michigan State University Museum

a dirt track. They rarely went to town.

Dr. Beal was a somber Quaker who never took a vacation. He never saw a play or played games.

The Beal house, though, was always full of exciting people. Many of the students came to talk about botany with her father. Other students came to see her mother, who "mothered" everyone who was sick, or homesick.

When President Abbot came to the house, he talked about stories and poetry. Dr. Miles talked about surveying. Dr. Kedzie talked about problems with food for livestock and arsenic in wallpaper. The professors ran experiments, and talked to the legislators, and got laws passed to make life better, safer.

> Dr. Kedzie helped set up the State Board of Health in 1873.

One of the students, Liberty Hyde Bailey, helped her father with his tests on plants. One time, Dr. Abbot asked if Mr. Bailey was a good student. Dr. Beal said, "With his curiosity, I suspect he will do something we have not even yet imagined."

> In 1885, Liberty Hyde Bailey started the first scientific program for horticulture in the country at M.A.C. He was Professor of Horticulture at Cornell University, New York, for many years. In 1993, the Children's Garden at MSU was dedicated to him.

In 1877, Dr. Beal began making tests on corn. In one year, he improved the corn crop by 50%. He wrote to Charles Darwin about his results.

– Michigan State University Archives

And then in 1879, when Jessie was nine, her father had another idea, for an experiment with seeds. He wanted to see how long seeds could live.

> This test resulted in our hybrid corn. The experiments on corn still go on today; look for the bags over the ears of corn at the MSU farms.

He told Jessie to bring the shovel. Dr. Beal and Mr. Bailey brought the 20 glass bottles. They had packed each bottle with 1000 seeds. Jessie helped them bury the bottles by a big rock on campus.

In five years, Dr. Beal would dig up one bottle, plant the seeds, and count the number that grew. In five or ten more years, he would dig up another bottle and see how many seeds were still alive.

He knew the experiment would go on long after he retired from teaching.

In 1980, 101 years after Dr. Beal buried the seeds, another bottle was dug up. Many of the seeds were still alive.

Botanists at Michigan State University plan to dig up the next bottle in the year 2000.

One of Dr. Beal's bottles,
dug up in 1980
– Michigan State University Museum

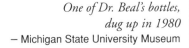

Many things were named for these men: Bailey Hall, Abbott Hall, Kedzie Chemistry Lab, and Beal Garden. In East Lansing, you will find Abbott Road, Bailey Street, Beal Street, Kedzie Street – and M.A.C. Avenue!

When she grew up, Jessie Beal married Ray Stannard Baker, a fellow student at M.A.C. and a nephew of Luther Baker. He won a Pulitzer Prize for his biography of President Woodrow Wilson.

One-Horse Sleigh

The teenaged boy was new in Lansing. He looked up and down the Grand River and tried to imagine the Great Ice Jam five years before, in April of 1875.

People said the ice on the river cracked and piled up very fast, with water still flowing under it. The ice pile moved downstream and slammed into a bridge. The bridge fell into the river with a great crash. Before the day was over, the river of ice destroyed five bridges.

It was a horrible mess, but the people simply built better bridges.

From the new bridge at Shiawassee Street, the boy could look down river almost to the dam, the place where towns always started. He knew the mills there had been a new idea forty years before. They used the water power of the dam to turn their mill wheels, the major change from Indian life to settler life.

The mills were even bigger now. Scofield's Mill stood where the first saw mill was built in

Great Ice Jam, 1875
– Local History Room, Lansing Library

1845. Mr. Scofield was making lots of wooden broom handles and felloes, the wooden spokes for wheels. The Carmer, Parmelee Mill had expanded, too, and was grinding lots of flour.

Parmelee Plaster Mill
North Lansing
– Local History Room,
Lansing Library

The boy had heard about the bad fires at the mills in the 1860s and 1870s. Men and boys ran to the river and formed bucket brigades to pass along water from the river. The engine company came with its little pumper, but it wasn't able to control such big fires. Mr. Scofield

Lansing's first fire engine, 1858 Button & Blake
– Terry Hinman

had to rebuild his mill both times.

The boy knew that, because of fires, the newer factories still had to be built near the river. They didn't have mill wheels, though, so they didn't have to be built near the dam. They used the river water in steam engines, which drove their machinery.

The boy heard the scritch of saws from the new Lansing Wheel Barrow Company. He could see the shell of the factory at Saginaw Street. They would build little wheel barrows to move manure in the carriage barn, and huge wheel barrows to carry luggage and boxes at the train station.

Investors were E.F. Cooley, J.H. Moores, B.F. Davis, and E.W. Sparrow.

And what a mess it was all along both sides of the river! Horses and wagons, stacks of lumber, junk, and rag-tag sheds were everywhere. The noise of people shouting, steam engines whumping, the smell of animals – not the best. And right in town!

Covered railroad bridge over Grand River, looking southwest
A bridge still stands on the original piers in Riverfront Park.
– Local History Room, Lansing Library

The clang of giant hammers pounding on iron came from E. Bement & Sons, a huge foundry on the west side of the river. Bement made pot-bellied stoves and iron plows. The iron plows were much better than the old wooden ones.

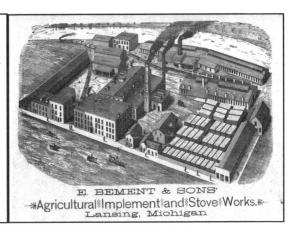

E. Bement & Sons
Bement made the first iron plows in Lansing in 1870. The factory stood on the site of the Ottawa Street Power Plant.
– Local History Room, Lansing Library

And now they built bob sleds! They sold as many as 10,000 bob sleds a year. The stoves, plows, and bob sleds made Bement & Sons famous all over the world.

Beyond Bement's, the boy could see the high school he attended, and the Opera House and Mead's Hall, where Mark

Bement Baseball Team
– Local History Room, Lansing Library

Twain once spoke. He could see the round tank for Mr. Cooley's Gas Light company. It produced gas for lights in houses and stores. People no longer had to use dim, smelly kerosene in their lamps.

Good ideas, he thought.

Buck's Opera House, built 1872
(Gladmer Theatre)
— Local History Room, Lansing Library

Lansing High School, built 1875
(Old Central)
— Local History Room, Lansing Library

A sleek rowing boat skimmed the water, moving very fast. He ran along the bank beside it, to the bridge at Michigan Avenue. The young men of the town practiced on the river for the races against teams from other towns. It looked fun. Maybe he would try that, too.

He heard the blast of the train whistle from the new depot, just a block away to the east. Now, the factories could load the trains with more and bigger products and carry them far, far away from the city. Quite a change from a wagon load of goods, pulled by horses.

As he thought about it, he realized that these new factories made only two or three products. They were growing very fast because of the trains – and because they specialized. *More good ideas*, he thought.

South of the bridge, at Washtenaw Street, he could see Frank Clark's father in the yard of his factory. He was checking over one of his beautiful wooden carriages.

Lake Shore & Michigan Southern Depot, built 1875
— State Archives of Michigan

It was a big business. Except for the mess and smell of the horses, the horse and carriage was the best way to get around.

If there was one more snow, he and Frank could use one of Mr. Clark's sharp little sleighs again, the one with pinstripes painted on the sides. The sleigh seated two people, and could be pulled over the snow by one horse. When the sleigh bells started ringing, everyone looked their way.

Sleigh
A. Clark & Co.
— Leland Knapp

He couldn't help singing the new song he had heard, "Jingle bells, jingle bells . . . ."

He looked farther up the river, toward his father's shop. He could almost see the sign, "P.F. Olds and Son." They built and repaired steam engines which ran little pumps or boats or other small machines. The "Son" in the company was Wallace, the boy's older brother.

The teenager on the bridge was Ransom E. Olds. The father said the boy kept daydreaming, tinkering around with things in the shop instead of doing his work.

It was true. R.E. Olds was daydreaming about carriages and steam engines and smelly horses.

R.E. Olds at age 16, 1880
– Pat Heyden

Another change was about to take place in our lives.

In 1886, R.E. Olds put a steam engine on a buggy and drove it through Lansing streets, an early "automobile."

Sources

Among the dozens of sources used for this book,
you will find the following especially informative and interesting.

Artifacts | Michigan State University Museum

Births, Deaths | Cemetery Records and Gravestones
& Marriages | Dep't. of Public Health, State of Michigan
| Newspapers

Property, | *Michigan Census Records*: 1840, 1850, 1860
Addresses, | City Directories, 19th C.
Jobs & Ages | Caterino, David. *Mudge's Directory of the City of Lansing 1878: Reprint.* HSGL 1991.

Histories | Adams, Franc L. *Pioneer History of Ingham County* 1923.
| Baker, L.C. *History of the Secret Service* 1867.
| Durant. *History of Eaton & Ingham Counties* 1880.
| DeLand. *History of Jackson County* 1903.
| Heyden, Patricia. *Metta and R.E. Olds: Loves Lives Labors* 1997.

Journals, | Mevis, Daniel S. *Pioneer Recollections* 1911.
Memoirs, | Moon, Darius. Woldumar, unpub.
& Genealogies | *Pioneer and Historical Society Papers* 1872- .
| Pioneer Family History Collection,
| Historical Society of Greater Lansing
| Potter, Theodore. *An American Adventure* 1913.

Maps | *Archaeological Atlas of Michigan* 1931.
| *Atlas of Ingham & Livingston Counties* 1859.
| *Indian Trails*. Michigan Historical Commission 1959.
| *Sanborn Maps*, 19th C. (Fire insurance maps which locate and describe buildings)

Photographs | Historical Societies
| Local History Rooms and Museums
| Michigan State University Archives
| Pioneer Family History Collection
| Private Collections
| State Archives of Michigan

Index

Index

About the Authors

Lori Heuft is a freelance writer and former legal secretary. Her past work includes articles in *Lansing City Magazine* and *Michigan Woman*. Lori and her husband, Jerry, are raising their three children in the Williamston area, where they have lived for over 30 years. They also have a horse, dog, and two cats. When she has free time, Lori enjoys helping with school-related activities.

Linda Peckham is a freelance writer, president of the Historical Society of Greater Lansing, and professor of English at Lansing Community College. Her publications include *The Pocket Hotline for Writers* and articles in professional journals and *Michigan History Magazine*.

She has written and spoken about local history for many years, served as Executive Director of the Lansing Capital Sesquicentennial in 1997, and recently provided local history resource material to teachers in 140 elementary area classrooms. Her husband, Robert Morris, is a historic preservation specialist, and they have two grandchildren in the local elementary schools.